DISCRIMINATED AGAINST BY RELIGION

Discriminated against by religion

ALDIVAN TORRES

Canary Of Joy

Contents

1

" Discriminated against by religion

"

Aldivan Teixeira Torres
Discriminated against by religion

Author: Aldivan Teixeira Torres
©2018-Aldivan Teixeira Torres

Aldivan Teixeira Torres is a consolidated writer in several genres. To date it has titles published in nine languages. From an early age, he was always a lover of the art of writing having consolidated a professional career from the second half of 2013. He hopes with his writings to contribute to the Pernambuco and Brazilian culture, awakening the pleasure of reading in those who do not yet have the habit. Your mission is to win the hearts of each of your readers. In addition to literature, its main tastes are music, travel, friends, family and the pleasure of living. "For literature, equality, fraternity, justice, dignity and honor of the human being always" is his motto.

" Discriminated against by religion

"

Final
End of First Mission
Conclusion

Carthage - Current Tunisia - year 465

Born a star of light in the beautiful dawn of Carthage, the current Tunisia. The Gordian Fulgêncio family had just received her first child on that fateful morning of January 12 of 465 A.D. and christened as Tales Cléber Gordiano Fulgêncio advised by the father Aristides who was Roman empire senator. The mother called Maria was also illustrious, belonging to a traditional family in the area.

It seemed possible that the child would have a wonderful life to be born into a wealthy family, acculturated and influential at that time still full of uncertainties and ethnic, cultural and religious persecution. At least that was what was expected. However, everything could happen and destiny was weaving invisible threads to that little life.

Shortly after birth, they hired for the boy a wet nurse, a kind of nanny that would meet every child's needs when their parents were fulfilling their long and everyday social commitments. Her name was Eva Ferrari and would work in the house of Fulgêncio family for six days a week earning the local minimum wage.

Besides the nanny, the boy won all the perks that their social status allowed: A specific bedroom fully equipped and a lot of love and attention of those who were around. Tales was really a lucky and special boy.

Let's go ahead!

Childhood

Tales had a normal childhood full of child's games, friends, trips, appointments together with parents, nanny, education and a lot of responsibility. Since early, he learned the true values of life including religious direction standing out among the other children of their age group. He was a boy of love.

By completing twelve years old, he gained more freedom in every way going to run the family estate with his father. At this time, the nanny services went dispensed and six months later, Aristides died leaving a fortune and the woman (mother of Tales) in the hands of the young boy. A decision from the young Tales was necessary.

With determination and courage, he faced difficulties and proved to be very competent in their duties. It's like the saying goes: "Iron and whip that build the man". Thus, was born the man "Tales", true fortress from Fulgêncio family.

The Monastery

From the age of 18, the range of social interests increased. In addition to the ordinary meetings of business and politics, Tales intensified their religious studies, art and literature which did achieve high public offices. He was appointed procurator of his homeland and tax collector. As expected, he performed his duties competently.

Tales also used to attend various living spaces to as being popular. Among the favorite places was the monastery. The monastery of Carthage was a very important religious congregation in the area. The goal of Tales to attend the establishment was a further clarification of the mysteries of the universe which he always questioned.

There, his main teacher was Gandarom, a secular leader who diffused all religions. One of the main meetings were discussed between the two interesting questions concerning the main issues of the time and that can be the same current in today's times. I transcribe below the main parts:

— Who is God, Gandarom? (Tales)

— It is the Alpha and the Omega, the beginning and the end, prior to all that exists. From the ground zero created and continually creates the infinite universe unreachable to our powers - he explained.

— What is God's religion? (Tales)

— Yahweh God is present in all religions. For nearly five centuries ago, he gave us one of his sons to serve as an example of conduct and uprightness. Yahweh wants us to be like him. (Gandarom)

— What's his name? (Tales)

— Jesus. (Gandarom)

— I see. My father told his story. It's really amazing. (Tales)

— Yes. He carried with our pain, our crosses and offered as atonement for our sins. He saved us - explained him.

— I knows. I've read something about. I just do not understand what moved him to this attitude. In my opinion, people didn't deserve and do not deserve this donation. (Tales)

— Truth. But wait. (Gandarom)

Gandarom got up and walked a few meters towards the library. Tales was to wait. In a few moments, he returned bringing with him a book and handed it to his disciple. then restart the contact.

— This Is the most important book in the world. Close your eyes and open a random page. It will respond to your concerns.

Tales did as suggest. When he opened his eyes again, faced with the following message: "The transgression of the wicked saith within my heart, that there is no fear of God before his eyes. The words of his mouth are iniquity and deceit: he hath left off to be wise, and to do good. He devised mischief upon his bed; he septet himself in a way that is not good; he abhorred not evil. Thy mercy, O Lord, is in the heavens; and thy faithfulness reached unto the clouds. Thy righteousness is like the great mountains; thy judgments are a great deep: O Lord, thou preserve man and beast. How excellent is thy lovingkindness, O God! therefore the children of men put their trust under the shadow of thy wings. They shall be abundantly satisfied with the fatness of thy house; and thou shalt make them drink of the river of thy pleasures. For with thee is the fountain of life: in thy light shall we see light. O continue thy lovingkindness unto them that know thee; and thy righteousness to the upright in heart. Let not the foot of pride come against me, and let not the hand of the wicked remove me. There are the workers of iniquity fallen: they are cast down, and shall not be able to rise." (Psalm 36, Holy Bible, by King James Bible Online)

The feeling that Tales felt then can be defined as elusive. There was the answer to all his life searches. God was so superior that he loved good and bad equally and without prejudice.

In a premeditated act, closes the Bible and say to the master:

— I want to renounce the world and find out about this unknown God. From now on, I will live a life of austerity and loneliness - decided.

— Have you thought of all the consequences? (Gandarom)

— I do not need to think. I just need to learn about this inexplicable thing that happened now. Wish me luck!

— Yes of course. Wish you find out what you are looking for.

— Thank you.

Said that. Tales withdrew from the monastery to start a new life. Concomitantly, the light in his chest begins to develop increasingly.

New Attitudes

After leaving the monastery, Tales sought to continue their activities. He continued perfecting himself at work and at home took care of the already elderly mother. He expanded his studies on religion, politics and relationships discovering every day new information. As he perfected himself, leaved a little aside the social life. The "things of God" became more important every day.

And so, in this rhythm of discovery took four long years. At the end of this time, he came to a conclusion: Your social detachment attitude and seclusion that devoted was not the answer to find the way. Despite their efforts he didn't reach the goal that was austerity, simplicity and encounter with God. What to do now? The only option he envisioned was to back to the monastery and reunited with Gandarom, his former master as needed his wise advice and guidance. Still pounded in his mind Psalm 36 messages that had encouraged the search: " ***Thy mercy, O Lord, is in the heavens; and thy faithfulness reached unto the clouds. Thy*** *righteousness is like the great mountains; thy judgments are a great deep: O Lord, thou preserve man and beast. How excellent is thy lovingkindness, O God! therefore the children of men put their trust under the shadow of thy wings."* He needed to find the thread and shelter on the strength of that unknown God who continually called him.

The Return to the Monastery

It was a calm morning at that January 12 of 487, a day after the firm decision of Tales. Soon early, after the completion of his morning activities and bid farewell to his mother, leave toward the outside of the house. In some instants he already was outside.

When leaving home, a veranda wooden chalet, headed to an attached stall which was on the right. With a few steps he reaches the place and begins to saddle his dear companion Protomeu his sidekick. When ready, ride on, gets out of the stall and win the streets of the great Carthage, an economic and political center of the time.

On the way, zigzagging on the streets, finds many acquainted and greets them with a nod. Didn't really worth depriving himself from the beauty of the world and the company of friends as he had done. He was sure that God did not want it.

Amid the expectancy, nervousness and anxiety he meets the route in thirty minutes. Drops, holds the animal in the shade of a tree and go to the destination gateway. It lacked little for another big step towards his restless life.

A few moments later, he finally arrives. He was in front of that door he had left four years ago with a decision. The turns life takes, the good son returns to the house and when he hit that door could rediscover their destiny and the master who thought all the time. Maktub! That God's will be done, he thinks and knocks on the door. Within seconds, it opens and from inside comes the enigmatic figure of his master wearing a white dress clothes, wearing leather sandals and appearing to be very good. With a smile he welcomes and invite him to enter. The old disciple accepted and then the two steps into the holy temple.

They went to a particular room and getting there, settle in chairs around a table, the only one fitment at that place. The master then faces the old disciple and could not contain his curiosity:

— And then, Tales? Did you find God in your gathering? Did that worth it?

— Yes and no. While I had time to reflect about the mysteries, I detaching myself a little from the reality of the world. In the end, I ended up not finding me. What do I do? Can you help me?

Gandarom frowns. With his experience, he expected that result and not only anticipated the disciple because he wanted himself the checked it out.

— Sure, Tales. In me you have a faithful friend. Yahweh God has a purpose in your life and think I am one of his instruments to make you see that. Look, I have a proposal. Would you stay here with me and learn a little more?

— I Want, but what about the rules? You know I'm not from royal lineage to have the merit of living in the monastery.

— I don't care about rules but you're right. I will consult my colleagues.

That said, Gandarom nodded and went out for a moment. Meanwhile, Tales takes and breathe all that air of tranquility and peace of the monastery, something he had not felt for a long time due to his long distance. It was really amazing.

Ten minutes later, Gandarom get back and through his appearance gave to predict what had happened.

— They didn't accept me, right? (asked the restless Tales).

— Exact. I'm disappointed with my brothers and I made a decision. (Gandarom)

— What? (Tales)

— I will leave here. I will go to another monastery here of Carthage, from the abbot Felix. If you want, you can come with me. (Gandarom)

— It's ok. Can I visit my mother from time to time? (Tales)

— Of course. We value the family. (Gandarom)

— So, It's Ok. I ask you to give me just a week to take care of business and prepare my mother for this news. (asked Tales)

— Make yourself comfortable. Meet me at this address within seven days - finished delivering a parchment manuscript.

The two-parted with handshakes as two gentlemen should do and finally separated. While one will pack the bag the other, as said, will take care of the last remaining details of his life.

Keep going always! In search of destination.

A Week Later

It passes another week and Tales complies with the agreement settling all your personal disputes. He had left the management of the business and the care of her mother to an aunt by the father called Rebeca. With her arrival, he felt relieved of their former responsibilities and could fly in search of new directions.

After pack up and a quick dismissal of the two, he routes to the stall attached to his residence. In moments, he is already in the place and immediately saddle your horse Protomeu. Getting ready, starts the journey, get out of the stall and win the streets of the troubled Carthage.

Facing traffic from other animals, Tales takes a delay to reach the final destination closed on parchment: The monastery whose leader was the abbot Felix. This was the friend that his master Gandarom use to spoken a lot. Arriving, keep the horse in a shade close. Who he would not split apart.

Facing the imposing building made from the most specialized architecture of the time with its columns, considerable width and height, its floating garden that housed a huge plant variety as well as sculptures and important paintings. That place was like a dream and Tales was hard to believe he had earned the invitation to live there and discover God through the people and not by loneliness as previously thought.

It had been a risk to get up there and since he had the courage would not hesitate anymore. He was going till the end even if the consequences were drastic. With this decision, he gives one, two... ten steps and then faces the huge gate. Now it lacked little.

In another demonstration of bravery, hit firmly at the door and only quiets when listening the sound of approaching footsteps. A few seconds later, the door finally opens. Inside the monastery, there was the figure of an also old man softly, white, thin and bald. With a formal aspect, he sees the visitor and says:

— What wants young? What is your name?

— My name is Thales and yours?

— Félix. Oh, you are my friend Gandarom's indicated. Come in, make yourself comfortable.

— Thank you.

Both enter inside the large building. Tales can soon see at first sight the charm and mysticism of that location. It was a nook where shelter saw all kinds of people: poor, rich, sick, stigmatized, acculturated and illiterate, as well as being a multi-ethnic and poly religious space. An ideal mixture to understand a little of God.

After overcoming the main hall, they go through two more corridors at right until they reach a reserved living room. There were all the assembled monks. When entering the room, he greeting everyone and went to talk specifically with Gandarom that was in the background. The meet between the two was exciting and rolls hugs, handshakes and kisses on the cheek.

At the end of this ritual, verbal contact can then start.

— So, you came? How nice. (Gandarom)

— I keep my promises. Now, I'm available. (Tales)

— Look, Felix, Tales is a young willing and wanting to find wise and understand the force that binds to our father. (Gandarom)

— Very good. From the beginning I realized that he has a special glow. Leave it to me. Together we will form the ideal spirit. (Felix)

— Thank you both. Whatever you need from me I'll be disposal. I am prepared to work, experience and above all learn. (Tales)

— Like that. We are really needing your help. See what's around us? There are hungry people, starving of the true spirit of understanding that we can provide them. You are one of the keys. Welcome. (Felix)

— If you need something particular, do not be ashamed. You can talk. (Gandarom)

— Do not worry. It's everything very good. I promise to fulfill my destiny. Where can I keep the bags? (Tales)

— Let me show you. (offered Gandarom)

The two leave the room, go through another corridor and has access to the block of dormitories. Directed to the bottom of which was already booked especially for the visitor. In a few steps, they arrive at the place, they enter, keep the bags and Gandarom suggests that the disciple rest in bed that was beside him. He accepted and lie down as the day would be long and require too much of his strength.

Meanwhile, work continued...

The First Lesson

Tales finally wakes up after about two hours of deep sleep. Immediately, get up, leave the room and seek for their masters. Go through the hallway, living room, more corridors and finally arrives in the first room, the lounge.

At this time has a vision of an unusual scene: A man flapping on the ground and the monks struggling to calm him. The scene gives him fear and prefers to follow by far the scene.

Fifteen minutes of intense agony where the situation is only controlled with great effort of Abbot Felix and Gandarom master. At the end, the man gets up and looks absolutely normal and fully recovered. He is then dispensed.

Right at that moment, Tales takes to approach and solve their doubts with the teachers.

— What happened here?

— was one demoniac - explained Gandarom.

— What did you do to calm him down? (Tales)

— We use the pray. It has the power to heal and cast out demons. (Abbot Felix)

— Teach me - asked Tales.

— You should pray, I command you, kind of demon in the name of our Lord Jesus Christ, to leave the body of this man and return to your hellish habitats. It was no accident that the Son of God gave himself on the cross and shed his blood for the remission of sins. Therefore, by his sacrifice, definitely get away to him and never return. Amen. (Abbot Felix)

— Jesus is one of two children of God, the other will be revealed only in the distant future - explained Gandarom.

— It's really amazing. This name has power and I really feel like calling me continuously to his breast - revealed Tales.

— So, deliver yourself, brother. I am part of this community. Feel free. (Abbot Felix)

— Thank you - said Tales.

— You have the right to choose. As in the past decided to retract now has the opportunity with us and the miseries of the world that we treat. We are the arrow showing the way, but the sovereign decision is always yours. (Explained Gandarom)

— You're right. Thank you for all the support, master. (Tales)

— You're welcome. (Gandarom)

— Let's get back to our obligations. (ordered the Abbot)

All obey and Tales is keen to help work with the sick people, in domestic activities and other related tasks. This way spends your first day in the monastery and he feels in a testing phase in his new life. A life illuminated by the spirit of love and understanding of the master.

Let's move forward.

The Work

The other day, since early, all the monastery wakes up and goes to do their morning activities. Specifically, the trio in question takes care of their short training. The day's lesson relates to the work and they endeavor to engage in full-time.

The main activities are: Bathing, prepare breakfast, eat breakfast, wash dishes, brush their teeth, clean the inside and outside of the monastery, walk around, shopping, prepare the budget, listen to music, read books, lunch, dinner and meet with the other members of the monastery in order to decide important issues. With this, the day was completed and the end the three were exhausted. What they wanted to show the disciple was that without work it does not get anything under the heavens.

The example of Persistence

Come to the third day of living in the monastery. After the ordinary activities of the morning, the three musketeers were meeting the need people that continually presented for them.

Tales was loving those altruistic activities. That made him feel useful to society. Exactly at ten o'clock in the morning, there was a middle-aged lady looking for Gandarom. She presented as Martha and seemed to have a special need; it was just a visit from an old friend who had not seen for a long time. Tales is kind enough to take her to meet him and causes a special moment between the two hugging each other for long.

The master then has a good idea taking advantage of the situation.

— Marta could tell your story to my friend Tales?

— Sure, he is a disciple?

— Yes, I'm - anticipated Tales.

— With pleasure. My name is Marta Gurgel, I'm fifty-five years old. I am a renowned businesswoman living a quiet life. However, it was not always like that. I've been homeless, maid in hotel, prostitute. On my own initiative, I sought to study and that's where our Gandarom friend enters in the story. He was one of my first teachers in the Central School of Carthage, we became friends and confidants. Despite all the difficulties, he encouraged me to fight for my dreams. That's when I had the idea of turning businesswoman. By the expense of my work, I opened a boutique in the suburbs. In the beginning, the movement was good, but over time has cooled and most of the parts that could sell was the term with bad debts in these cases nearing thirty percent. Result: I broke. Helped by Gandarom, I did not give up and kept fighting for my projects. And all attempts were seventy resulting in failure. In the number seventy-one finally found something that identified me and everything went swimmingly. Today I have my network of furniture stores. What I learned through the master is that we should never give up the goal, persist is the key to success.

— Amazing! Congratulations! I do not know what to say! (Tales)

— The example of Marta can be applied to any situation. We are all capable. (Gandarom)

Felix Abbot arrives and also intervenes in the conversation in order to give good news:

— Companions. I decided. From now on, you will be the leaders of the place. You have shown enough capacity to do so.

— Congratulations! More than deserved! (Marta)

— I don't know what to say, thank you, friend. (Gandarom)

— Me? I'm not just a disciple? (Tales)

— I've been watching their movements in these three days. You and your master are the most suitable for the office. And if you allow, I'll baptize you in Christ Jesus. (Felix)

— I wants. Right now. (Tales)

Felix Abbot walked away for a moment, returning shortly after with a water-filled basin. With the help of Gandarom and Marta performed the ritual consecrated Tales to Christianity. Now the Holy Spirit could act fully in his life.

After the ceremony, Marta said good bye and the three musketeers were taking care of their respective daily activities. The time was pressing.

The Period of Six Years

After appointment, Tales and Gandarom started a wonderful job with the monastery. With innovative and insightful ideas, they made Felix's abbot' Monastery a center of excellence in charity, advice and guidance for people of all ages. Allied to this, he increased in wisdom, joy and happiness with his study about the Christianity.

However, not everything was rosy. The fifth century was a period of repression and persecution for those who accepted the Christ through the authoritarian politics of Transmudo King. He tried in every way to demoralize Christians

The apex of persecution occurred on that fateful December 15 of 492. When going to shopping, Tales and Gandarom were arrested by guards at the behest of Transmudo. They were tied up, humiliated and taken to prison. Once there, they were beaten and tortured in order that denied the Christian faith. However, they remained firm in the faith and eventually being released.

When they returned to the monastery, they organized a meeting to make a final decision. That situation could not last.

Forced Travel

The outcome of the meeting decided the future of Tales. It was decided that he would withdraw from his functions and would travel against fellow monks in the Egyptian desert. It was needed to give a time once Carthage became increasingly dangerous.

Taken the decision, our august personage immediately went to prepare the details of his departure. He packed a bundle of clothes with personal objects and named someone to replace him in his work at the monastery.

With everything ready, he took his favorite horse Protomeu and took his journey towards the coast where the ship would take him toward the final destination. As Carthage was by the sea the distance from where he was would be covered in a short time.

So, it does. In forty-five minutes from fast gallop, he arrives at the port, let his friend Protomeu at the care of a commissioner, walks a bit and up the boarding stairs on the ship that was about to leave. Fate was released.

Twenty minutes later, the ship departs and at this time Tales is in one of the rooms on the ship with all the comfort available at the time. As that was his first trip at sea, He felt a little sick and unwell, but nothing to take away their faith, determination and hope for better days.

He takes advantage of the time available, sits on his bed and begins to read his inseparable Bible in the part referring to the Psalms. Focus his attention to the following passage: *"Do not fret because of those who are evil or be envious of those who do wrong; for like the grass they will soon wither; like green plants they will soon die away. Trust in the Lord and do good; dwell in the land and enjoy safe pasture. Take delight in the Lord, and he will give you the desires of your heart. Commit your way to the Lord; trust in him and he will do this: He will make your righteous reward shine like the dawn, your vindication like the noonday sun. Be still before the Lord and wait patiently for him; do not fret when people succeed in their ways, when they carry out their wicked schemes. Refrain from anger and turn from wrath; do not fret—it leads only to evil. For those who are evil will be destroyed, but those who hope in the Lord will inherit the land. A little while, and the wicked will be no more; though you look for them, they will not be found. But the meek will inherit the land and enjoy peace and prosperity. The wicked plot against the righteous and gnash their teeth at them; but the Lord laughs at the wicked, for he knows their day is coming. The wicked draw the sword and bend the bow to bring down the poor and needy, to slay those whose ways are upright. But their swords will pierce their own hearts, and their bows will be broken. Better the little that the righteous have than the wealth of many wicked; for the power of the wicked will be broken, but the Lord upholds the righteous. The blameless spend their days under the Lord's care, and their inheritance will en-*

dure forever. In times of disaster, they will not wither; in days of famine, they will enjoy plenty. But the wicked will perish: Though the Lord's enemies are like the flowers of the field, they will be consumed, they will go up in smoke. The wicked borrow and do not repay, but the righteous give generously; those the Lord blesses will inherit the land, but those he curses will be destroyed. The Lord makes firm the steps of the one who delights in him; though he may stumble, he will not fall, for the Lord upholds him with his hand. I was young and now I am old, yet I have never seen the righteous forsaken or their children begging bread. They are always generous and lend freely; their children will be a blessing. Turn from evil and do good; then you will dwell in the land forever. For the Lord loves the just and will not forsake his faithful ones. Wrongdoers will be completely destroyed; the offspring of the wicked will perish. The righteous will inherit the land and dwell in it forever. " (Psalm 37.1 to 29)

Tales thrills. These words of comfort were perfect for the critical moment that he was living. Yes, he had faith, trust in God, in his providence and overcome all the obstacles that were placed in his Follow-Christ activity. No one had the power to take off his happiness achieved through the son of God who continually called. And that Maktub! Accept his plan with serenity.

After reading the text, he closes the Bible and aims to make a tour on the ship. It would be good to get to mingle with other fellow travelers. Aiming at this, get out of his room and wins the side of the ship. With this, have the opportunity to meet other travelers with their fate, each one with its history and private life. At the end of this exercise, has resulted in the consolidation of several friendships. It was exactly what God wanted him unlike his previous gathering.

Two hours later, he is back to his room and took the opportunity to rest a little. After all, the trip would be long and exhausting. While relaxing, if inebriated by the beauty of the giant sea in front of him with its natural beauty. Everything he was really living was spectacular even though admittedly sad to have to leave his monastery class who had much esteem. But he had no way out.

Time passes slightly, the afternoon progresses and the night comes. He's activities range from dinner to attend a rapid little party with local singers. This made a lot of good for your heart who was indeed anxious, fearful and distressed. Later, going to sleep and tries to do it the best way possible.

Goodnight to everyone.

Stop in Syracuse

Dawns after a troubled night full of nightmares for our beloved Tales. It had not been easy the first experience under the sea for obvious reasons. It was a critical moment in every way due to the change of life.

Aided by his natural clock, he wakes up with a superhuman effort can finally lift. The first thing he does was to go to the toilet, take a good bath and relax a bit. Then, out of the shower, change clothes and forwards to the kitchen to taste the pleasures of the meat.

With quick steps, he does everything quickly and arriving at the place it seems that was not the only one because the restaurant was crowded. Still, he could find at the background a table with a single person and there he goes.

He finally settles down. Educated as he was, ask excuses for the person presents and assesses the menu. Asks for something simple and while the food doesn't arrive, he starts chatting with the girl called Cruzes about general subjects and about themselves. It's like the saying goes, evangelize always choosing not date or time.

Ten minutes later, the food comes, he starts to eat but still interacting with the girl who was very friendly. In this short time, they get as friends. At the coffee end, they say goodbye, revise the latest recommendations and finally get back to his room. Oblivious to all this, the ship continues its march in invisible.

As the day before, he gets to rest and observe the movement of ocean waters through the window of his room. In this observation, he learns other meanings than those he already knew in the monastery such as the transience of things and uncontrollable fate that persecuted him. However, he was resigned and asked for their prayer's serenity and faith face to everything that was happening.

About an hour later, the ship stops and it draws the attention of Tales. He leaves the room, walks in the main car and realizes that anchored in the port that by his calculations would be the port city of Syracuse. The goal was to replenish the fuel in order to complete the entire path.

At the anchored moment, a man entered into the ship and began to shout from the rooftops:

— Egypt is in turmoil! The Church of our Lord Jesus Christ cannot steady because of intense internal conflicts. Therefore, those seeking refuge in Egypt must rethink.

That said, he left the ship without saying goodbye to anyone. To our dear traveler, that was a sign. Certainly, that man was an angel sent by God and there was still time to reconsider. Intuitively, he made a decision: He turned around, returning to the room. quickly packed his suitcase, went down the ship and got to expect a ship headed back way. He would return to their land that however bad it was still had their who to trust. Would face your reality without running away and that was what God wanted.

Back Home

Two hours later came a ship whose destination was the intended. Immediately, our august personage hastened to pay the ticket, boarding and accommodate at a room available. The adventures would restart, but in the opposite direction.

A few moments later, it's already started the journey taking our friend dreamer, a perfect follower of the laws of Christ and because of this was pursued. Would face them! Would back to the monastery, would expose his arguments and expect the support of his friends. Hope that it works!

Meanwhile, he tries the various distractions: Read the bible, wander the various compartments of the ship, watching the sea, lunch, dinner, talk, rest and meditate. Everything was very intense and pleasurable due to the expectation back together in their monastery that he already considered a family.

At the end of the night, they already reach the end point: The wonderful and impressive Carthage. Full of happiness, Tales descends from the ship bringing their bags, ambitions, fears and concerns. Soon at the land, rent an available animals and firm part toward the monastery. That Christ gave him luck and blessing.

On the way, he has the opportunity to revisit places. This was his city that even with its problems was beautiful, attractive and hospitable. The challenge was to get along with some people, prejudiced antichrists and inhuman that did not respect the choice of others. These do not have the name written in the book of life as they are beings without soul.

Thirty minutes after departing from the port he already reaches the destination. It is exactly 11:30pm and he had no other choice than to try to wake up his fellow monks. Face to the main gate, he tries once, twice, three times. At last, he gives a shout and finally he hears noises. Someone approached.

From inside the establishment, leaves an armed person till the teeth and this fact scares him. Notes better and notes that it was abbot Felix. Tales comes to be identified in order to prevent further tragedy.

— Calm down, Abbot. It's me!

Felix struggling through that half-darkness. Find out the identity of the figure and then crack a smile.

— Tales? Is that you? What happened?

— Yes. The Egyptian church is in conflicts. I had no choice but to return. Could you accept me?

— Of course. I wouldn't refuse to receive you at this hour. Tomorrow we can talk better.

— Thank you.

Felix gives way to Tales and the two steps into the monastery closing the door behind them. Guided by Felix, he goes to the same small room that previously occupied and getting there, seek to sleep. The day had been quite busy.

Decision II

Comes a new day in the great Carthage, geopolitical and financial center of the time, was the seventeenth day of December 487 and the morning seems calm and cozy. Early, as usual, everyone rises and Tales was no exception despite all the fatigue that brought from the trip.

Fulfilling the daily routine, ending at breakfast and after that they set an urgent meeting in a private room between them except Tales. In an hour of intense debates define the fate of that which had led that institution for nearly six years.

Finally come to a conclusion and chosen to convey the news was the wise, beloved and eternal master of Tales, the Gandarom. He leaves the room and went to the room where the disciples had settled.

They are the hardest steps of his life to take, but extremely necessary. As get closer, Tales realize the desolation of the master and has a bad intuition.

— Tales?

— Yes?

— The council met and decided on your departure. I'm sorry. For them, you became a danger.

— Me? I don't even hurt a cockroach.

— You know what I'm talking about. The antichrists are increasingly active and pressuring from all sides. I do not agree, but there is nothing to do. The majority wins.

— I understands. I will leave. First, however, I wanted to say that you are special in my life. You, your company, advice, and experiences helped me all this time. You were a second father. Thank you very much.

— You don't have to thank. I also learned a lot with you because nobody knows everything. Look, when you want to visit us, feel free.

— Thank you.

— Where are you going now?

— I do not know. I'll go home and see if tidy my ideas. I'm only sure about one thing: From Jesus Christ I don't separate myself more even if it costs my life.

— I give you all my support, I will remember you in my prayers. Good luck.

— For you too. A big hug.

— See you.

The two greet each other with handshakes as the usual. Gandarom escorts him to the exit. The still young Tales disappear on the streets of the big city. Life sets ways for the two. Although they have different destinations, each one would carry the other in the chest for the entire life.

At Home

Tales walk through the streets of their city full of anguish, fear and nervousness. At that moment, he felt a big pain in the chest by all recent events. Was practically expelled from the monastery and from the life of your friends just by doing good. Even being aware that it was not their fault, she felt unprotected and abandoned as his master on the cross.

Now only had himself, his spiritual father and his aged mother who visited there a while. It seemed little, but was still in better condition than most people. At least he had health to work and his faith remained firm ready for new challenges.

Thinking about everything, makes a balance of the pros and cons of their decisions and finds that life immersed in the gospel was really special. He had opportunity through its activities to help people of all genders and classes. Thus, meet the following saying: "We are all equal before the father".

Even in a difficult time, not thinking about giving up his mission, "voices of light" who still called him to do good. Should exists a way to overcome this momentary disappointment and keep on going. He just had no idea how to do this now simply because was very upset. The best was to rest for a while.

Firm on this decision, it hastens the steps, zigzagging through the streets in order to be distracted. A little later, finally reaches the final destination, feeling at home, go through the stable and there was his old friend Protomeu, embraces him and gives him a quick brushing. Then leave the place and goes to the door of his residence and as the fact that it was ajar just makes a push.

The first thing he sees in the room was his mother resting on the chair. She seemed to be so concentrated that does not realize his presence. He gets thrilled because his mother was amazing. Also, by being that housed for nine months in her belly and fed, and only by this fact demanded unconditional love of him.

Discreetly, hisses and this makes the mother drive the vision in his direction. When crossing glances, an unfathomable mystery of love is realized and they are in microseconds properties in contemplation. After this time interval, they come into contact.

— Tales? Is that you, my son? You remembered your mother?

— Yes, it's me, mom - he said moving closer.

She has no time to get up. The child comes close to her and gives a warm kiss on the forehead.

— Came to stay? (She Question)

— I came give time to myself. Do you accept me?

    — How do you ask me such a thing? I'm your mother. My love is immense and without restrictions.

— Thank you. And my aunt Rebeca? Where is she?

— Went to shop. She'll be back in a little while.

— Is that really you? How are you doing?

— With the grace of God, Mom! And you?

— The same. My age does not allow much anticipation.

— Come on, Mom! You are still very young.

— It's your eyes, my son. But I am resigned. I thank God for all that he gave me even for having a son like you.

— Thank you, mom. I thank him for your life. Is there something to eat in the kitchen?

— Yes. Scrambled eggs.

— A delight. I'm going to eat. We'll talk later.

— Be my guest, son. It's your house.

Tales went to eat because he was hungry. Once there, it does not take more than fifteen minutes to replenish forces. After that, keep bags, went to talk again with his mother and in the meantime Rebeca arrives. They greet each other with euphoria and continue to interact. They had to take this time that life had given.

Then take a shower, go out to the streets a bit and only return for dinner. Then lock himself in him room, read the Bible and try an illumination. Unsuccessfully. Later, tired, went to sleep. The coming days promised.

The Week

Weekdays go by and Tales takes this time at home to help rearrange things. Among the main activities, business visits, tour and reunion with old forgotten friends, Bible studies, investigation of antichrists, in addition to caring for the mother, the most important thing in his life. He was living a divider point of water, where practically anything could happen for good or evil. It was up to him to use the right tools to achieve success.

At the end of the week, after all the marathon previously mentioned activities, he sat down and reflected on the most important aspects related to his life and of the family. Getting to an important conclusion.

In view of this, at a Sunday afternoon, approached from his mother and went to her a final conversation. She was in the room taking a nap in her favorite chair. To get close, he woke her gently up and the two could come face to face in a frank conversation.

— What do you want, son?

— I was thinking one thing and wanted to consult you.

— So, tell me. I'm listening.

— Mom, do you know me like no one else. I'm still a young man full of dreams and challenges, with achieved values. You also know my instinct for freedom, creative and insightful. I came to a decision.

— I understands. You are trying to tell me that you are going away again. Is that right?

— Yes, and not only that. I also decided to sell my part of the share of the property and build my own monastery. Jesus calls me in mission.

— Are you sure?

— The only certainty I have in life is that, beyond death of course.

— So, I approve it. Go get in your missionary work the essence of your life. However, do not forget your old mother -she recommended.

— Certainly. I'll visit you when I can. Give me the blessing, my mother.

— I bless you in the name of the father of the two children and the holy spirit.

— Amen.

Tales retires and go take care of some details. Already had someone in mind to sell their properties, assisting people and a specific location to build the headquarters of his project. With his mother's approval, he would settle in person.

No later than three months longer he wanted to be installed and working. Would call the monastery as "home of the resurrection," an allusion to that master performed every day in your life and in the issues of the planet in general.

Good luck to him!

Some Time Later

The time progresses. Thanks to his personal efforts and some friends invited, Tales realizes his ideal founding the home of the resurrection in 80 days, twenty days ahead of the schedule. In order to commemorate the event, he organized a small party, with the confirmed presence of singers, pipers, people of the Christian community, family and friends to be held at the project headquarters.

It was the sixteenth day of March 488, a quiet night and average brightness of the great Carthage. The "Home of Resurrection" was close to downtown and with it the mobility of the guests was facilitated. Exactly at 8:00pm, event time, everyone we were already in place and this fact has brought much joy to our main character. Jesus was actually leading this great crossing which was shown ahead of his beginner life.

Making the role of host, Tales begins the festivities. The special night is surrounded by music, entertainment, candid conversations between groups of people participating, food, drink and an atmosphere of great peace.

One hour after the beginning of the party, someone knocks at the entrance gate of woodsy cottage, 15x8 meters dimensions divided into six compartments: two bedrooms, main hall, kitchen, library and unloading bay. Tales went personally verify who the intruder in order to take a final decision. Hoped it was not an antichrist because if it was, even being for the peace side he would have to react and fight for their rights of religious choice, something still not complied at the time.

In a few steps, already comes to the door and opens it abruptly, he prepared for the worst. What he sees causes laughter crisis. The person who knocked at the door was nothing less than his eternal master Gandarom.

— What is so funny? (Inquire Gandarom looking a little dull)

— Nothing. I was thinking foolishness. But get inside. The house is also yours.

— Thank you.

The two steps into the monastery and go join the other partygoers. On the way, full of curiosity, our august character does not hold and start the conversation.

— How did you know?

— One of our mutual friends told me and I could not resist. It's everything very beautiful, congratulations!

— Thank you. Feel free.

The party continues with the joy of all participants. Everyone who was there, one way or another, were part of the dream of Tales, a dream of communion, interaction, tracking the Christ and the good values of life. A dream that was realized in joining forces. It was people like him that the world needed.

The party follows until 11:00pm. As a farewell, Thales proposes a prayer: *"Hear me when I call, O God of my righteousness: thou hast enlarged me when I was in distress; have mercy upon me, and hear my prayer. O ye sons of men, how long will ye turn my glory into shame? how long will ye love vanity, and seek after leasing? Selah. But know that the LORD hath set apart him that is godly for himself: the LORD will hear when I call unto him. Stand in awe, and sin not: commune with your own heart upon your bed, and be still. Selah. Offer the sacrifices of righteousness, and put your trust in the Lord. There be many that say, who will shew us any good? Lord, lift thou up the light of thy countenance upon us. Thou hast put gladness in my heart, more than in the time that their corn and their wine increased. I will both lay me down in peace, and sleep: for thou, LORD, only makes me dwell in safety"*. (Psalm 4)

Everyone repeats and applaud. That prayer was the essence of the priestly mission, which at that time was shrouded with danger. It was necessary to the high strength to not give up or falter. Because only the Lord and his two children could save, protect and ensure the continuity of the mission.

With the end of the work, everybody bid farewell to leaving Tales alone. He would try to sleep in peace with God without major concerns. From the other day, would give the kickoff to their jobs counting with his three friends help: Peter Pedra, Angelo Mussolini and Rita Andrade. The first would be an Abbot and the two other assistants.

Let's move forward.

The Mission

The day after the inauguration, " Home of Resurrection" began its altruistic activities. Similar to another monastery that Tales had conducted there was no differentiation between people, all denominations who needed help could participate.

Tales and his friends mentioned above had to solve a variety of problems range through advice, guidance, and giving education on a scale of relay so that the institution would work all day.

Initially few visits, their work was released gradually through word of gossips and then in less than a year they already had to schedule the service. Sign that the work was being recognized, Tales considered an angel of light: spokesman of spiritual forces called "voices of light" which meant his obedience to his father and his two sons.

Nomination

After two years of work commanding the "Home of Resurrection", the name of Tales gained much notoriety in Cartago region. The information of his work came to the bishop Gurgel Fontes that after a brief analysis decided by his nomination as a priest of Christ's ministry, linked to the Catholic Church.

Tales was immediately notified of the decision and accepted by free own will the new denomination. He committed for at least three times a week to deliver sermons, worship and preaching in order to garner more faithful to Christ. However, not abandon his work in the monastery because his essence of life, austerity and simplicity was in this.

Good luck to him!

Trip to Rome

Tales began his priestly activities a week after the appointment. With his charismatic, polite and persuasive way drew crowds to worship. The message conveyed was that God was father and together with his children called everyone for a change of life: Forgo the world of sin, deliver his cross who could carry and renew itself with the power of the holy spirit.

Parallel to this work, he also still served the monastery helping sick, oppressed, depressed, unbelievers and foolish and the most hardened sinners. It complies to the following word: "Through my children, I will find the lost cattle of my flock"

With a year of dedication to the two activities, there was an invitation from Rome to submit their work to the pontiff and he did not think twice and accepted it. It was an honor and a dream to have the opportunity to meet the Pope St. Felix in person.

Decided, Tales took care of the last outstanding issues: Recommendations on the monastery to his friends and the request of a priestly activity license. Regarding this last item, succeed at the same time. After, he packed a bag containing personal items of basic necessity.

At the next day, with everything ready, he sealed his inseparable horse Protomeu and went towards the local port. Galloping at a good speed, reaches the final destination (the port of Carthage at the time was quite busy) overcoming common obstacles of a big city of the time: Animal traffic coupled with the lack of planning of the streets. But survived, left the animal in the hands of commissioner that would take him back home and left now wait for the ship that would take him to Rome, the world center of that time.

While waiting, pulls conversation with others who also waited for the ship and not lose the opportunity to preach about Christ and his mission. Thus, gains the sympathy and admiration of most people.

Forty minutes later finally arrives the ship, a queue of passengers in order of arrival is formed and one by one going up the stairs that connect the port to the anchored vessel. Approximately in the middle was our character and up the stairs while straightens his clothes and his hair that was a little messy. No harm was to have a bit of organization and self-love.

All board. After getting the keys to the employee of the carrier, Tales drives to his accommodations, the first room on the right, and as it was well located do not delay to arrive. Inside the room, keep bags and took the opportunity to rest a little. Moments later, it is given to departure.

So started a new journey in his life and he hoped that this time was happier than the last time. As the vessel moves forward, our beloved character unfolds in various activities. Bathes, walks, makes a quick snack, read some bible and tidy your room. Later, lunch, dinner, help in washing dishes and preaches his religion to his fellow travelers. Everything is going swimmingly nor costly crossing of the Ocean was fatiguing him. As advanced night, he goes to sleep.

About 01:00am, Tales wakes up startled. What was happening? The entire ship rocked so he thought that it would turn. Immediately left the comfort of his bed and went to check what it was in the master's room. For this, he runs through the skeleton of the ship - Checks a taken rays' environment, lighting, constant rain and filled with terrified people - till he arrives where it was located the room. Entering the room, talk to the driver and is informed by him that are facing a dangerous storm and perhaps wasn't secure to continue in the way. Tales is amazed and moved. How that could be the end? He could not believe that his plans and even their lives were in danger because he was young and had a lot to accomplish and win in every way. That's when inspired by the Holy Spirit uttered the following prayer: *"I invoke you, the Lord of hosts. You who with a mighty hand delivered Israel from Egyptian bondage and God their children magnanimous, became fruitful barren woman, changed times, calmed the lions. I ask you another prodigy who is to let us free in this stormy weather through the merits of your children. Amen"*.

After repeating the prayer three times, blew a fine breeze on the ship and slowly torment passed. All then reassured and admiration were to greet the man of God. Tales began to teach them:

— Do you see brothers? Yahweh is the true God. He considers us children and never forsakes us, even in larger trials. The only thing he required is that we follow his commandments and we respect your children's authori-

ties. It is written that thou shalt not kill, thou shalt not steal, thou shalt have no envy, greed or slander, not to discriminate, be humble, charitable and generous, you shall love the Lord your God with all your heart, to your brothers as yourself.

— Who are the children of Yahweh? (Someone in the crowd asks)

— *The Body Son of God is called Jesus Christ and is the master that I follow. However, there is a spirit whose coming on the earth will occur in a distant time. It is he who will judge us with a rod of iron and bring peace.*

A law doctor who was present on the boat moved closer and stared at the speaker, taking the floor.

— The Scriptures say is Jesus that will return to earth if I'm not mistaken.

— *God has its secrets. This spirit child of which I speak is to come is the essence of Jesus, the Father and the Holy Spirit, forming one being. So, whatever we call it Jesus, Yahweh or his own name. The scriptures are right - explained Tales.*

— It means that the Holy Trinity is unreal? (Continued Gervásio, the lawyer)

— *It's not about this. Each one believes what is convenient for you. The truth is that Yahweh God is light, love, divinity and spirit and is present in pure and undefiled hearts. This is "The mystery of communion" and that cannot be understood by humans. God is omnipotent, omniscient and omnipresent - finished.*

Before that caused greater controversy, Tales retired and was trying to sleep. others did the same. When he arrived in the room, lay down on his soft bed and looked thoughtful for a moment. What made him say those words? He impressed with his boldness in demystifying concepts so broad. However, do not regretted. Continue to be bearer of this inexplicable force that moved him, "The voices of light continue with their sovereign will held". A moment later, he fell asleep and forgot all worries packed by comforting dreams.

The trip continued the following days and Tales continued distracting is the best possible way. Luckily, there was no damage and all arrived in Rome at the tenth end first day of travel. Berthed safely and immediately our august character arrives, rent a horse, ride carrying his bag and follows course of the local ministry. Now it lacked little to make one of his biggest dreams.

Passing through the main streets of Rome, Tales is delighted with the architecture, trade, the landscape and the people's way. No wonder that Rome was the center of the time. The only sad thing was prejudice and blind persecution of members of his religion.

An hour later, arrives at the destination, drops from the horse, asks permission to enter the complex showing his letter of recommendation and be given the passage tying the animal to a tree located in the garden annex.

After, accompanied drives the inner courtyard of a servant. Overcoming natural barriers, they have access to the anteroom, living room, hallway and finally the private room of Pope St. Felix. The servant retires, he knocks on the door and the pontiff went to answer. The white old man, low, medium and bald stature, wearing costumes sleeping, meets with a smile on his face.

— You're Tales?

— Yes. It's me. I just arrived of the trip.

— What glad you came. Come in. Let's talk.

— Thank you.

Tales enters the room and with a sign went to sit in the pope's bed that was next to a sort of nightstand. On the right was a chest and a writing table that had ink and scattered leaves. The Pope sits next to him and starts the dialog.

— I called you because I wanted to meet you in person. Came to me the rumors of your beautiful priestly and charismatic work in front of a monastery. Could you give me more details?

— I'm Just a servant of the Lord. Everything I do is driven by him. I accepted the priesthood because of that I would have a greater opportunity to redeem Christ to souls. He wants everyone and especially those who are away from their presence. With regard to work in the monastery, it is a large work, difficult but rewarding. I consider myself a bearer of good news.

— Very well. I wish they were all like you, willing. Have you thought about expanding this work?

— Yes. However, it is not simple. How the Lord knows the persecution is constant and many still lack the courage to face the central power. I understand you.

— Said the master: ***"Whoever seeks to preserve his life will lose it and who lost it by my name, there will to meet it".*** We need to follow this.

— I agrees. Difficult it to convince others to do so.

— Sure. But we need to propagate it. Do you allow me to use your example as inspiring model?

— Yes of course. It is an honor.

— So, it is so agreed. Now tell me, how is the beautiful Carthage? How was the trip?

— Normal. With all common problems of a big city. In relation to travel, we had setbacks but we won.

— Thank God. Our father is wonderful. I was praying for it.

— Thank you. I always had a curiosity. How is like to be Pope?

— It's a great mission. I have all the world responsibility in my back having to look after the interests of Christ and the Church. Every day, I have to take final decisions.

— Damn! Very impressive.

— Would you like to be the pope one day?

— No. I love the Church, Christ and the father but I like my life, my work and I know I would have to give up everything to take over this function. It is not written!

— *(It's true, is not written)*

— *(I am happy with this)*

— Very well. Now I will leave you. It's late and we need to sleep. Tomorrow you will have the whole day to visit Rome and have contact with people.

— Thank you very much. It was a pleasure to meet you.

— Equally.

The two embraced and in this wonderful moment Tales felt intoxicated and understood why he was the pope. After the embrace, become separated, the servant returned and walked Tales to one of the chambers, a central bedroom. At the place, the first thing he did was keep your bags and plummet in bed. The other day would run fast and he would have to recover the detached forces on the long journey.

Walking in Rome

The day soon came. After a meal and quick bath, Tales came out to the streets of Rome accompanied by a local priest named Giancarlo Fontana. On horseback, began to go visit the main points of ancient Rome Pantheon, the Roman Forum, the Coliseum, the Arch of Constantine, the Palatine, the Circus Maximus, the Baths of Caracalla, some squares, trade and lastly, tombs of the apostles.

In the latter, he felt the local mysticism strength groaning is enough. What the "voices of light" informed was that in them lived the great love of God for having loaded size and burden faced the authorities of the time. The persecution to the church were much higher then.

At the end of the day, they returned to Episcopal and tried to rest. The other day, new decisions would be taken.

The Return

The following day, early, there was a brief meeting between the members of the clergy and the visitor and then he was released to return to his duties in his land. He immediately tried to say goodbye to everyone and packed his bags.

With everything ready, he took his horse and headed toward the port. On the way, facing the traffic of animals and people, the supervision of the Roman guards and this slows down a bit their arrival at the final destination. Arrives in the time limit, let the horse with the commissioner port and start up the long stairs and at the end of it embark. Inside the ship, is approved by the company's attendant carrier handing him the keys and walks about the room, there are a few more steps to find the site and into the same, he sleeps in his room guarding the bags and resting on his beautiful bedroom. Minutes later, it is given to departure. Begins the great crossing between the two continents, Europe and Africa, which was expected to last about 11 days.

Helping the good weather and the calm waters of the ship made its way ahead without major problems. Tales took advantage of the free time to make friends, to preach, to further their studies and reading, join the festivities it was also the son of God. Every moment was important and our beloved character was well aware of that. As the days passed, he was convinced that his way was with the public, in the simplicity and austerity. A lesson learned.

At this rate, the eleven days passed quickly. Arriving at the port of his beloved Carthage, he went down carrying their heavy suitcases. Rent again another horse, saddle and ride, starting immediately toward his dependencies, the "Home of Resurrection." At the moment, he feels accomplished, met the pope, increased his network and heal some of your questions crucial. Now there was only to continue work together with his devoted friends.

Carthage had not changed. It was still a mess of people, religious denominations and political authorities to face. The challenge of Thales as a priest and man was to reconcile their mission with advertising. Everything had to be done as discreetly as possible because otherwise his claims could be aborted early.

Aware of this, we strive to not be noticed. Within fifty minutes is back to the monastery. then takes his master key, opens the door and goes to his quarters. As it was night and was very tired, just have to even go to sleep and dream about new achievements. And that's what he does. Enters the room, throw the bags into a corner and falls on bed. The other day return the horse promising more action in their simple life.

Tales, the new Bishop of Ruspe

Spending another year and reached the year 492. Each day, advancing projects of our beloved main character becoming known both in Carthage, whole Tunisia and all the limits of the Roman Empire.

Parallel to this, increased the persecution of Christians taken by the highest political authorities. The king of Carthage, the Transmudo, went so far as to order that there were no successors to the deceased bishops. His goal was to quench the Church.

A reaction on the part of Christians was organized. In a meeting held in Rome, they decided to thwart the king's order and elected sixty bishops. Tales was one. Named for the city of Ruspe.

After the decision, it was sent a communication to each of the chosen signed by the pope recommending not to refuse the job. Otherwise, they were collaborating with the objectives of the infidels.

Arriving the communication for Tales, he was divided between the flattery of such a high position, fear and concern for the faithful. He decided to think about that a moment later because of the personal commitments he had.

However, everything was about to change.

The Exile

In less than a week, rumors that new bishops were elected reached the ears of the oppressor. The fact that they have become even more anger with the Christian denomination. Their first act was to call the officers of the guard and ordering the arrest of all involved and subsequent exile of convicts.

And so, happened. The guard of Transmudo's king was behind every bishop elected and when met all together escorted to a shipment towards the Italian island of Sardinia, belonging to their domain. They did that to be respected and no more contradicted by the Christian denominations.

So that was his tyranny right in the V. century, but even he couldn't be more than God. Could only act as far as he was allowed.

The Crossing

It was April 04, 492, a fateful date where about sixty bishops were being pushed, humiliated and demoralized to the public by royal guards in the port of Carthage. One by one, were forced to enter an old vessel commanded by men of knew cruelty and rigidity.

The bishops were divided into ten rooms, six on each. The hygienic conditions, food and treatment were poor, only supported through prayer chains. However, anyone complained about their fate. They would go till the end by Christ as he had done biggest thing for them.

Thus, remained the martyrdom of Christ's followers during the five-day trip. Unfortunately, not everyone could handle the situation and died from grief and hunger. Their bodies were thrown into the sea. The other survivors began to consider them heroes and Christian symbols of resistance.

At the end of the five days, the survivors disembarked and were allocated a provisional arrest in the city of Cagliari. It was a maximum-security prison where Christians would be subject to the rules of the infidels. And then? What would be for the Christians and their evangelization of claims? Let us wait the next chapters.

Letter to the King

The Cagliari Prison conditions did not differ from the ship that brought the bishops. It was an environment with low light, full of rats and cockroaches, overcrowded and with God's people fighting for space with serial offenders.

Willing to change this situation, they exchanged messages with each other choosing Tales as a spokesman to be the most astute and enlightened of the group. The idea was to sensitize the king and achieve better conditions for all.

The first idea that the man of God had been to send a letter to his Royal Majesty. For that, he took a clean parchment, pen and ink in your suitcase began to write his letter. below:

Cagliari, April 10, 492

To Transmudo the king, lord of Carthage

Cartago - Royal Palace - Africa

Subject: Reconsideration

Tales, Christ's servant and representative of the exiled bishops in Cagliari, comes through this ask your excellency a reconsideration of the unjustly imposed conditions to our Mother Church and all who are here through the grounds specified below.

We, as servants of God, we come to the limits of the humiliation: We were disrespected, battered, treated like animals and pushed against a ship without any conditions of transport. We suffered hunger, thirst and anguish not knowing exactly what was going to happen. Arriving on the island, we continue with the same problems, and imprisoned as criminals and joined together with them.

With all due respect, Your Honor, we are not equal to the last! We are a legion fighting for humanitarian work involves counseling, treatment, donation and profession of our faith. If there is respect on your part and from many we ask at least understanding and justice.

We are aware of our rights, especially freedom and if the injustice that's being committed remains, we'll until the last consequences in the Roman courts. But this wouldn't be necessary. I know your insight, intelligence, reason and appeal for our dignity and freedom. May the Lord enlighten their decisions.

Sincerely and with all due respect, Tales, the man of God.

Cagliari, Sardinia island - Roman province

When finished the letter, Tales handed it to the officer and now remained only hope. The die was cast.

Repercussion

Five days later, the king received the letter. Read it carefully and in every line was more impressed. Who was that man who said so beautiful and brave words? Without a doubt, even if he was insensitive, he could not remain indifferent to so constructed request. That's when a glimmer of light, ruled in favor of the bishops.

He took a scroll, ink and pen and wrote an order to the authorities of Cagliari, the island of Sardinia. It was the freedom of the bishops, the construction of a monastery and the permission of the profession of faith of the same at least in the region where they were. The order was to take place immediately.

After he sent the letter by one of his officers. Ready! God showed up by a bully and this was a sign that he was on our side of our beloved Tales.

Three Months Later

The king's order arrived the following week. As ordered, began the construction of the monastery and arrest the bishops began to be better treated. Meanwhile, they continued with his studies and prayers permanently.

Exactly three months later, on 17 July 492, the monastery was completed and then they were released from prison and housed there. At their first meeting, they chose Tales as general manager of the site for its persuasiveness, kindness and sympathy.

So then initiated a new phase in the life of fifty-five bishops.

The Sequence of Work

Tales and his faith fellow began altruistic activities of the monastery. Similar to the work done in Ruspe, the place was open to all denominations which led the Tales of work to highlight throughout the Roman Empire. He became professor of bishops, writer, priests' faithful monks and a peacemaker of controversial issues before the rulers and the general population. He became a born leader recognized even by kings.

It was through his priestly activity and his literary work called "Answers to the ten objections" which was a replica of the orthodox issues that earned him a travel invitation to a brief return to Carthage. In order he wouldn't want create conflict, Tales accepted the invitation to the debate.

It was the holy spirit acting through people extolling the work of our beloved Tales placing him among the greats. He was a symbol of controversy, wisdom, unity, faith and especially of love among the lowliest. Someone worthy of the high-power lighting "from voices of light" that continually called and inspired him.

Soon after his decision, he packed his bags, leave from their jobs a while and went towards the port of the island of Sardinia that would take him to his beautiful Carthage, a land he much loved.

In Carthage

The trip between the island of Sardinia and the great Carthage was within the normal range except an engine problem that was quickly fixed. At the end of the fifth day, they landed in the port. As usual, Tales rented a horse already sealed. He rides up and set off into the royal palace.

While rapidly traverses the congested streets, he thinks of his mission in the family that has long not seen, and in the power and influence of the tyrant. He really had no choice but to attend to their private meeting and that "Voices of Light" put their exact words in his mouth.

Yes, he was prepared for what came! With the experience gained at the height of his 27 years he had already assimilated the peacemaker spirit, creative and patient. *(He was the right man for the occasion)*

Was within this spirit that he with courage and faith come into all the distance that separated him from the enemy's stronghold. He put the horse in the shade and stopped in front of the giant Roman architecture building with two floors, fifteen compartments thirty meters long by twelve broads, yet composed of garden, two internal walls and seven towers. Now was the time to the Jaguar drinks water.

Bringing together the latest forces he approached the gate where there were two guards manning. He introduced himself, mentioned the reason for the visit and then one of them accompanied him to the inside.

Overcoming natural obstacles of the way, both have access to the inner courtyard, go through two corridors with rooms on either side, go up the stairs, access the first floor through four compartments to reach the real hall. At this point, the guard leaves him alone. The king was distracted and just turns his attention because of the sound of footsteps. Then comes into contact as the visitor comes closer.

— Tales? You here?

— Yes. Come meet your Royal call. What do you want?

— I know about your work and wisdom. I want to put you faced to the Aryans with the intention of a clash of ideas.

— It's ok. When will it be?

— Later. For now, it is better you to rest. The journey must have been long.

— Thank you.

— Xerxes come here shouted Transmudo shaking a bell and thus causing a high-pitched sound.

Within moments, a thick mulatto, low, muscular, about forty years entering the royal dependencies. With a sign, he accompanied Tales of the guest rooms located on the same floor. The first thing that the servant of God did was undressing and plummet in bed. Transmudo was right, he was exhausted and would want to fully recover as the next act promised enough emotion. He sleeps immediately.

Passed over two hours. Tales wake up to someone knocking on the door of his dormitory calling him. With a spectacular jump up out of bed, dress and promptly went to answer. It was Xerxes again.

— Transmudo calls you for a hearing at the religious temple. The Aryans arrived.

— It's ok. Let's go.

Tales accompanying Xerxes. Pass through the royal hall, the corridors and rooms go up the stairs toward the second floor. The effort unfastened in the ascent does both quite transpire.

At every step, the expectation increases for our dear character that already planned all in his mind. The most important was not to lose control, education and decency in this type of meeting where *"the opposite face up"*.

At the end of the climb, they stop a bit and regain their breath. then resume the walk, they enter the second floor and consequently the temple which was the only compartment from above.

The king and two Aryans who were known as Arthur François and Tête Perré already waited exactly in the center. Xerxes says goodbye and then Tales advances alone toward the tormentors. While staying very close, they greet courtesy and the King starts the conversation.

Well, gentlemen, as we all are present, I think we can start our interaction. I emphasize that the meeting is purely friendly. The greatest interest is the friendly clash between ideas aimed at learning their different dogmas and worldviews. According?

— Yes. (Everyone agrees)

— First Question: What is religion to you? (Transmudo)

— Religion derived from the term "religare" which means reconnecting. That's exactly what the man seeks since it is in the face of the earth, a connection with a higher, inexplicable force that we call God. (Explained Tales)

— Religion Is any particular view of the world and seeks to unite with the Creator. Aided by its precepts and by faith we can achieve the union with the divine. (Artur)

— Religion is the way we use to explain the universe, ourselves and the creator. It is the invisible thread that unites us to him. (Tetê)

— It's ok. But what do you preach? What is really the truth? (the King)

— God is legion. Commonly attributed to his figure to the father, son and holy spirit. But the truth is that the Lord God is a whole present in all the pure hearts through the communion phenomenon. This is why Jesus said, *"I and the Father are one"*. (Tales)

— Blasphemy! The father is one and cannot be compared to anyone. (Artur)

— For us, Jesus was the son, but without sharing with the same substance of God. (Complemented Tetê)

— What if I told you that Jesus is not the only son of God? (Tales)

— How is that? (amazed Artur)

— I don't think so. (said Tetê)

— The discussion is getting interesting. Continue. (Intervened Transmudo)

— Yes. Jesus is the body son, born from the Virgin Mary. But will come another, the spiritual son, who will bring justice, peace and understanding to the globe. He shall feed his flock with a rod of iron.

— How do you know? Where does it say that? (Artur)

— I do not think so. (Repeated Tetê).

— *"Just as people are destined to die once, and after that to face judgment, so Christ was sacrificed once to take away the sins of many; and he will appear a second time, not to bear sin, but to bring salvation to those who are waiting for him".* (Heb 9.27 to 28). Who has ears to hear, let it be heard?

— I never had seen this text this way. (Confessed Artur)

— Me neither. (Tetê)

— Need to have intelligence for that. Congratulations, Tales, you have my admiration. (Transmudo)

— Thank you. (Tales)

— And about to what you preach? What man must follow? (asked Transmudo)

— The ten Commandments. (Artur)

— And The theological virtues. (Complemented Tetê)

— Not only that my friends. (Tales)

— What else then, the smarter one? (Artur)

— *So Says Jehovah, Yahweh, Oxalá, Jesus, Emmanuel, Messias, Christ, the son of God who are "the voices of light": "Hear, Israel, the West and the East people, my name is Yahweh, perfect and multiple, omnipotent, omniscient and omnipresent. I am the same from beginning to end and do not change. However, you have created for me a role of a cruel God, vengeful, authoritarian and prejudiced which is not consistent with reality. On the contrary, I am the power of love in a broad sense that you have never experienced except through my children. And you wonder: What must follow then? I am the way, the truth and the life and say, "You shall love your God, yourself and others above all things; Thou shalt not lie; shall not slander; no evil shall speak of thy neighbor; No shall cause intrigues; shall not assaulting; Do not offend your neighbor; fair headquarters, magnanimous, generous, compassionate, gentle and perfect as your father; Thou shalt not steal; shall not rob; not will practice larceny; Thou shalt not wear any kind of drinks or drugs; Do not covet or fall deep in gambling addiction; Be tolerant, understanding, patient, peaceful and human as well as my beloved children; Do not envy before work and fight for their goals. I do not forget anyone because for everything under heaven there is the right time. Avoid loneliness and sadness because I created you to success and happiness; Avoid prostitution, immorality, adultery, incest, and all sexual perversions for ye are the temple of the holy spirit; Ye are brethren. Therefore, we demand unity and cooperation for the common good; deliver his cross to me and renounce the whole-body illusion. I'll be ready to listen to them and promise dedication to your cause. I am kindly asking you this because the day thief is something you do not know. Finally, I say I love you and always believe there is a way out. I have faith in man as much as he does not deserve". (Tales, inspired by the voices of light)*

— A Broader explanation of what Jesus told us about love. (Found Artur)

— Exactly, My dear. In this we agree. (Tales)

— Great. Like that. You have my admiration. (Transmudo)

— And what you say atheists? The pagans and worshipers of other sects? (Tetê)

— *"The spirit blows from there to here, but we do not know where it comes from or where it goes." Lord God is multiple and in one form or an-*

other are present in all denominations. He is the Lord of the spirits and the forces of good and evil have to pay him homage. (Tales)

— Makes sense. (Tetê)

— So, as I understand it, there is one God regardless of denomination there are several ways to get to him. (Transmudo)

— Yes. As the saying goes, be part of a religion does not guarantee salvation to anyone. What guarantees are the good deeds, words and actions on the globe. (Tales)

— Wonderful. Very well. Finally, what message you would leave me?

— *Listen O king the God of Israel and the whole world: "As you rule over our people, I rule over the seven heavens. Whatever you do here on earth is being recorded, measured and sifted so that when the time due to pay the account settings. I recommend the practice of justice, understanding and tolerance that has long life and success on earth. Remember: I am the Lord; I see everything and no good man to conquer the world and lose your soul. So, what is a man to offer me in exchange for your salvation? For me money, honor and glory are mere earthly illusions. What I want are pure hearts, contrite and honest".*

— I ask for more freedom and respect to our beliefs. (Artur)

— I want to be happy without fear. (Tetê)

Transmudo blushes and seems to have liked what he heard. Immediately, it comes in contact with a serious and rude tone of voice:

— It's ok. I've heard all you had to talk. Now get out, you are exempt.

Tales and others obey without flinching. It was the best thing to do as the king was the type of person who could not face or counter. While the first down one floor and go to the bedroom to pack others are directed again the stairs that would lead them to the ground. They would take care of their respective churches.

In the bedroom, our beloved character takes no more than thirty minutes to take a shower and pack his things. At the end, he leaves the room, goes through the royal hall, bids farewell to the king and servants and finally goes away. Get the horse and rides again.

Initially aimlessly, decides to go to his mother's house to visit her and sleep as the night found himself early. And so, it does. Crossing streets to the right and left, greeting acquaintances, revisiting important places he comes home exactly at 10:00h. Keeps the horse in the stable and heads to the front door.

Faced the door and beats then twice until someone comes answer him. This is your Aunt Rebeca and they two greets each other with hugs and kisses. Speaking softly, she explains that Mrs. Maria is asleep and cannot be bothered. He understands the two steps into the house and he heads to his old bedroom.

There he keeps his things, lies down on the bed and try to sleep after a day of intense emotions. Let's move forward.

Return

The night goes by quickly. It begins to dawn; dawns and our dear bishop awakes after a night tormented by nightmares. Phew! Says relieved. Do their morning prayers, gets up, stretches, bathes, takes his suitcase out of the bedroom, he comes into the room and talk to her mother. In short greetings and conveys the importance it had in his life. After, says goodbye, go stables, rides the horse and goes in search of the continuity of his worship in Sardinia.

He was ready! The last experience showed that he was close to discovering his father's strength, of the "Voices of Light" that constantly blessed and directed the minutest aspects of life. He felt, therefore, blessed and loved by his father, by his master Jesus and all his brothers in the way.

Believer also increases the animal gallop and in thirty minutes arrives in the busy port. Drops, delivers the animal to a responsible and wait a bit. It was about 7:40am and just at 8:00am a ship would be dock toward the island. He takes this time to reflect, pray and be ordered to God.

The ship arrives at the expected time. Tales climbs the steps of the port, boards the ship, talk to the attendant and followed by him goes to be installed in one of the bedrooms. This time, he would have to share the place with three people because the stocking was complete.

Moments later, it is given to departure. Would be five long days crossing the ocean and that promised much excitement because of the time lately was cloudy. He would have the time to read, eat, work and make friends with roommates and travel and this was very helpful for all that he represented. He was the man of God, spokesman of light.

The trip is shown busy. The ship stops twice by technical problems, along with his group they dive six times in the sea alternately occur festivals, debates, crises, quarrels, orgies, rumors and bad storytelling. Some of these things makes Tales want to get right to land and others to stay. It is the famous dichotomy represented by the "Opposing Forces".

With half a day late, they finally arrive. After landing, the bishop drives to Cagliari where his brothers were waiting for him anxiously. There's about more thirty minutes again on the back of a horse.

Facing the monastery, he sent the horse back and carrying her backpack knocks on the door. The first time, already heard steps in his direction and then wait to be answered. It was exactly 12:00pm when the door opens and comes from inside one of his brothers, Bishop Francisco. After the usual greetings, the two steps into the building, and while the brother keeps his belongings in their bedroom, he went to have lunch. After, rest and late in the afternoon resumed work as a bishop and as monastery manager. At night, dinner, meeting and more rest. And so, life went on with the blessing of God.

Ten Years Later

The Tales works and his brothers continued. Every day, they reached more prestigious on the island and throughout the Roman Empire although the time of persecution had not ceased due to the prejudice of many. But they were warriors and winners.

In his intellectual work as a writer, Tales stood out again with the work "Three Books to The Transmudo King" that condemned the Arians practices which yielded a new invitation to return to Carthage in which he did very well by the way. The man of God then broke more barriers giving a notorious example of enlightenment and wisdom.

A while after this second visit came the king's death news. The oppressor was dead, and things could change. Keep watching, readers.

New Position

The new king of Carthage was chosen and took possession. His name was Hilderico and unlike Transmudo had a more liberal and tolerant spirit. The first important decisions taken was: financial reform, review of political alliances and decision by the return of the exiled bishops.

Achieved by this decision, Tales and his friends prepare for the return. Closed the monastery in Cagliari, they packed their backpacks and left the next day from the port of the island towards the great Carthage.

With this, a new direction and a new mission was prepared to their lives together in their homeland.

In Ruspe

Soon after arriving in Carthage, the bishops were divided in their respective dioceses. As expected, Tales was sent to Ruspe and together with the pope's help began to organize a wonderful job. Shared their daily activities in the religious and humanitarian administration.

Already well known, was wanted by the people to solve any problem and with the right words and attitudes comforted and guided. It was a true father to all the community.

Allied to this, he continued his work as a preacher, Christ religion diffuser, combatant of heresies and writer. which in comparison said with the congregational authorities threatened to withdraw to Circinia in case he was not met their demands. They then did not allow and reforms were made size was his power of persuasion. Regarding types of works, he wrote another book, a treatise on unbaptized children and became a theological model. He became so an example for the entire Christian world.

And so, time passed up swiftly.

Final

The weather continued to advance. The church expanded, persecution continued, close people died (the mother of Tales Mary and her Aunt Rebeca), the work was increasingly recognized getting a taste of more wants, loneliness and indecision about the future. The only certainty was that he had wanted to surrender to the divine power and the voices of light have chosen him from birth to a life of simplicity, austerity and above all love for the faithful and brothers of all denominations.

As performing their daily work in a simple life, as stated earlier, Tales died on January 1st 533 at sixty-eight years old. His body was buried inside the church where he worked. With his death, stays the example of struggle, unreserved surrender to the father, example of human being inspired by "Voices of Light" that so many refuses to listen. Keeps the message: "Although the man fall is not fatal because the Lord sustains him with his hand", that is, we can stumble, tremble before the great challenges of life, but if we face with determination and faith on him who can give us victory, certainly we'll be big winners. "Do not fear because I have overcome the world".

End of First Mission

The vision ends. The four friends (Baltazar, the Seer, Emanuel and Messias) who were at the cross of the giant Poço da Cruz dam decide to return home because the related mystery "to the voices of light" was completed and explained.

With this decision, drives to the VW old Beetle, step into and run toward the village. There were many tasks to be carried out. Traveling at an average speed, that result in only ten minutes away.

As they drop off the old Beetle, say goodbye and each one follows their ways. In direction to the respective residences. As everything in Jeritacó was too close everything is very fast.

The scene is now fixed at Mr. Messias shack. The three have just arrived, the Seer go pack his bags and as completes it finally reached the moment of separation of the three loyal friends. The Seer comes into the living room and contact with others.

— Well, I'm going now. Thank you both for everything. It was a pleasure.

— The Pleasure is all mine, young man. When you want, stay with us. (Messias)

— Thank you. (The Seer)

— I cannot accept it. You are very special and I always have you with me. (Emanuel)

— We'll be always together through the power of light. This is the mystery of communion. We are all one. (Aldivan)

— He's right, son. In addition to that we'll see each other more often. Our series is going to be successful, isn't it Seer? (Messias)

— Of course. I hope so. I already have a title for it: "Voices of Light." (Aldivan)

— Sounds good. We also want to thank your presence. Go with God, son of God. (Emanuel)

— Amen. (The Seer).

The three embraces. By those three beings had been done a deeper mystery than our vain philosophy could imagine. They were a set of spirits ready to transform the world and the universe through his adventures.

At the embrace ends, the Seer moves to the exit, open the door and before crossing it completely listens to a last warning: "Beware of trucks!" He laughs. That was really an extraordinary coincidence or not knowing Emanuel at such a critical time. He would thank him for his life forever.

The Seer finally comes out. Walk a few steps and looking for a public phone and when he finds links to Wellington and combine it come and get him. He waits a while.

Two hours later, he arrives, they greet the Seer carrying his suitcase, enters the car and is given to departure. He would soon be back to his land. That new adventures comes on.

Conclusion

I want to first thank all the readers and admirers of my work who were willing to read the entire book. It is for you who I give myself every day with professionalism, safety and truth.

I hope that the end has been a little of what I wanted to pass on: The example of faith, claw, altruism, of selflessness in helping others. Let us be like Tales, light bearers that can always illuminate our spirits. A good luck to everyone, happiness, success and see you at the next book if God permits.

End.